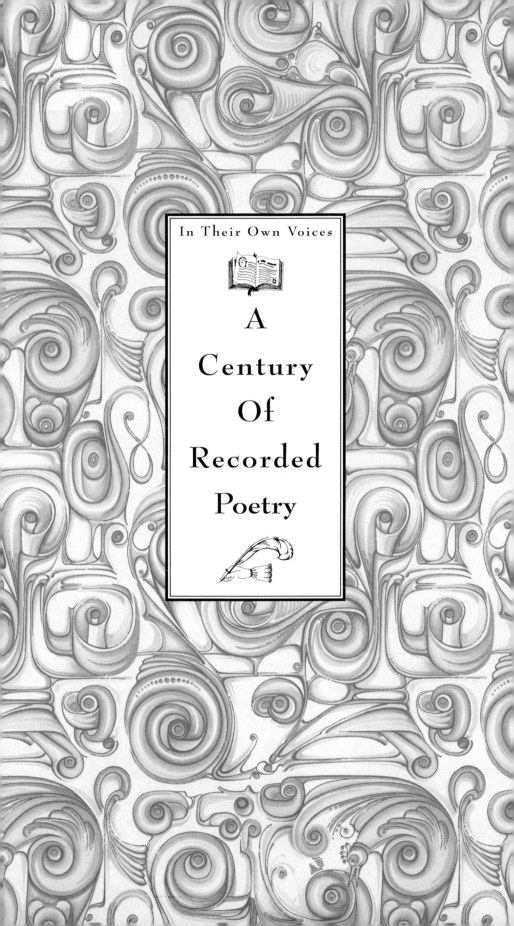

In Their Own Voices

A
Century
Of
Recorded
Poetry

Compilation Produced for Release by:
REBEKAH PRESSON & DAVID McLEES

Project Supervision:
TED MYERS

Research Assistance:
BRUCE BERLIND, PATRICK MILLIGAN

Project Assistance:
ROB COHEN, ELIZABETH PAVONE

Licensing:
MARK PINKUS, STEVE POLTORAK

Remastering:
BOB FISHER/DIGITAL DOMAIN

Art Direction:
COCO SHINOMIYA

Design:
GIRLWHOFALLSDOWN

Illustrations:
JASON RAINEY

Photos:
DOROTHY ALEXANDER & ARCHIVE PHOTOS

Special Thanks:
JESSICA RENAUD & ED FOLSOM/
Walt Whitman Quarterly Review,
PROFESSOR LOWELL CROSS,
MICHAEL B. YEATS, JOE BERK,
DAVID McINTOSH

The Production Department (Brian Schuman, Rick Brodey, Norma Edwards,
Nancy L. Hopkins, Tom Eckmier, Bill Inglot, Chris Clarke, Stacy J. Santillan,
Angelica Khoylow, Julie Temkin, and Allyson De Simone) wants to thank you for
picking up this fine piece of audio product. (What do you think? 1-800-546-3670.)
We're the folks that proof the liner notes, prepare the print, track down the masters,
put them on tape, and finally manufacture and ship the goods . . .
all to get this disc safely into your CD player.

SUGGESTED READING:

Like the Beat Generation before them, a new generation of young American
writers has emerged from the coffeehouses throughout the nation. *Caffeine* magazine, a
Los Angeles bimonthly, has been documenting these writings since 1992.
Scream When You Burn (Incommunicado Press) is the new anthology featuring
the best words from the first three years of *Caffeine*. Writers in this anthology
include Charles Bukowski, Pam Ward, Lyn Lifshin, Rick Lupert, Sandra Mizumoto
Posey, and Andrienne GreenHeart, among others. For more information,
call (213) 468-1250, write to P.O. Box 4231-306, Woodland Hills, CA 91365,
or email poetrymag@aol.com or check out the new words (or post your own)
at http://www.hallucinet.com/caffeine.

SUGGESTED VIEWING:

Be sure to watch PBS's *United States Of Poetry.*
For more information call 1 (800) 647-3600.

Other Titles From Rhino/Word Beat You Might Enjoy:

CHARLES BUKOWSKI: *Hostage* (#71758)
WILLIAM BURROUGHS: *Call Me Burroughs* (#71848)
ALLEN GINSBERG: *Holy Soul Jelly Roll - Poems And Songs (1949-1993)*
[Box Set] (#71693)
JACK KEROUAC: *The Collection* [Box Set] (#70939)
KEN NORDINE: *Word Jazz, Vol. 1* (#70773)
VARIOUS ARTISTS: *The Beat Generation* [Box Set] (#70281)
VARIOUS ARTISTS: *The Cowboy Poetry Gathering* (#71573)

VOLUME ONE

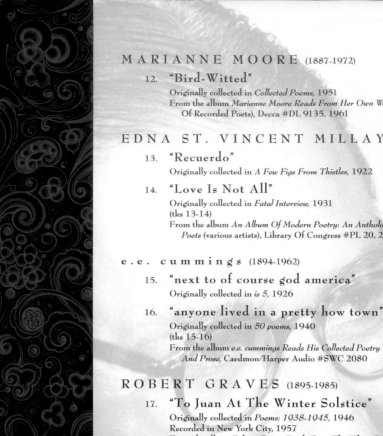

Ogden Nash

Theodore
Roethke

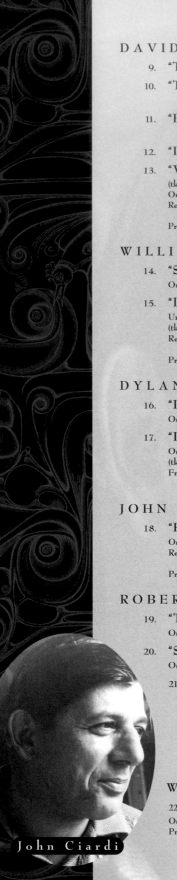

John Ciardi

LAWRENCE FERLINGHETTI (1919-)

23. "See it was like this when..."

24. "Underwear"
(tks 23-24)
Originally collected in *A Coney Island Of The Mind*, 1958
Recorded at The Writer's Center, Bethesda, MD
From the album *Lawrence Ferlinghetti: Into The Deeper Pools*,
    Watershed Foundation #C-167, 1984

CHARLES BUKOWSKI (1920-1995)

25. "The Secret Of My Endurance"
Originally collected in *Dangling In The Tournefortia*, 1981
Recorded at the Sweetwater, Redondo Beach, CA, April 1980
From the album *Hostage*, Freeway #1058, 1985

HOWARD NEMEROV (1920-1991)

26. "Thanksgrieving"
Originally collected in *Sentences*, 1980
Recorded in Kansas City, MO for broadcast on the radio program
    New Letters On The Air, 1990
Previously unissued

MONA VAN DUYN (1921-)

27. "Sonnet For Minimalists"
Originally collected in *Near Changes*, 1990
Recorded in Kansas City, MO for broadcast on the radio program
    New Letters On The Air, 1991
Previously unissued

RICHARD WILBUR (1921-)

28. "Shame"
Originally collected in *Advice To A Prophet*, 1961

29. "Apology"
Originally collected in *Advice To A Prophet*, 1961

30. "Love Calls Us To The Things Of This World"
Originally collected in *Things Of This World*, 1956
(tks 28-30)
From the album *Richard Wilbur Reading His Poetry*, Caedmon/Harper
    Audio #SWC 1248

JACK KEROUAC (1922-1969)
With Al Cohn & Zoot Simms

31. "American Haikus" (Excerpt)
From *Book Of Haiku*, an unpublished collection, portions of which appear
    in *Scattered Poems*, 1971
Recorded in New York City, 1958
From the album *Blues And Haikus*, Hanover #5006, 1959

LISEL MUELLER (1924-)

32. "Monet Refuses The Operation"
Originally collected in *Second Language*, 1986
Recorded in Kansas City, MO for broadcast on the radio program
    New Letters On The Air, 1981
Previously unissued

ALLEN GINSBERG (1926-)

33. "America"
Originally collected in *Howl And Other Poems*, 1956
Recorded at Town Hall Theater, Berkeley, CA, March 1956
From the album *Holy Soul Jelly Roll: Poems And Songs 1949-1993*
    (box set), Rhino/Word Beat #71693, 1994

Lawrence
Ferlinghetti

9

JOHN ASHBERY (1927-)

34. "Song"

Originally collected in *The Double Dream Of Spring*, 1970
Recorded at the Library of Congress Recording Laboratory, Washington, D.C., 1973
From the album *John Ashbery: The Songs We Know Best*, Watershed Foundation #C-230, 1989

GALWAY KINNELL (1927-)

35. "After Making Love We Hear Footsteps"

Originally collected in *Mortal Act, Mortal Words*, 1980
Recorded in New York City, 1996
Previously unissued

36. "Last Gods"

Originally collected in *When One Has Lived A Long Time Alone*, 1990
Recorded in Kansas City, MO for broadcast on the radio program *New Letters On The Air*, 1981
Previously unissued

VOLUME THREE

W.S. MERWIN (1927-)

1. "The River Bees"

Originally collected in *The Lice*, 1967
Recorded in 1970
From the album *W.S. Merwin Reading His Poetry*, Caedmon/Harper Audio #CPN 1295, 1970

JAMES WRIGHT (1927-1980)

2. "A Blessing"

Originally collected in *The Branch Will Not Break*, 1963
Recorded at the Poetry Center of the 92nd St. Y, New York City, 1976 & 1977
From the album *The Poetry And Voice Of James Wright*, Caedmon/Harper #SWC 1538

ANNE SEXTON (1928-1974)

3. "The Truth The Dead Know"

4. "All My Pretty Ones"

(tks 3-4)
Originally collected in *All My Pretty Ones*, 1962
Recorded in 1974
From the album *Anne Sexton Reads Her Poetry*, Caedmon/Harper Audio #V 1441

MAYA ANGELOU (1928-)

5. "Phenomenal Woman"

Originally collected in *Phenomenal Woman*, 1994
From the album *Phenomenal Woman*, Random House #387, 1995

RICHARD HOWARD (1929-)

6. "Even In Paris" (Excerpt)

Originally collected in *No Traveller*, 1986
Recorded in Saratoga, NY for broadcast on the radio program *New Letters On The Air*, 1989
Previously unissued

ADRIENNE RICH (1929-)

7. "Diving Into The Wreck"

Originally collected in *Diving Into The Wreck*, 1973
Recorded at the University Of California, Santa Cruz, 1986
From the album *Planetarium: A Retrospective 1950-1980*, Watershed Foundation #C-201, 1986

Photo © Dorothy Alexander

W.S. Merwin

DEREK WALCOTT (1930-)

8. "Omeros" (Excerpt)
   Originally collected in *Omeros*, 1990
   Recorded in Kansas City, MO for broadcast on the radio
   program *New Letters On The Air*, 1990
   Previously unissued

GARY SNYDER (1930-)

9. "The Song Of The Taste"
   Originally collected in *Regarding Wave*, 1970

10. "How Poetry Comes To Me"
    Originally collected in *Left Out In The Rain*, 1986

11. "Why I Take Good Care Of My
    Macintosh Computer"
    Unpublished
    (tks 9-11)
    Recorded at the Capitol Hill Hotel, Washington, D.C., 1989
    From the album *This Is Our Body*, Watershed Foundation #C-231, 1989

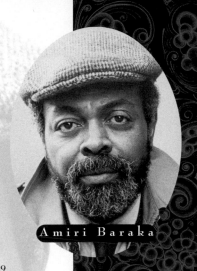

Amiri Baraka

SYLVIA PLATH (1932-1963)

12. "Daddy"

13. "Ariel"
    (tks 12-13)
    Originally collected in *Ariel*, 1965
    Recorded in London, October 1962
    From the album *Plath Reads Plath*, Credo #3, 1975

DAVID RAY (1932-)

14. "The Greatest Poem In The World"
    Originally collected in *The Tramp's Cup*, 1978
    Recorded in Kansas City, MO for broadcast on the radio program
    New Letters On The Air, 1979
    Previously unissued

JOHN UPDIKE (1932-)

15. "An Oddly Lovely Day Alone"
    Originally collected in *Facing Nature*, 1985
    Recorded at Updike's home, Massachusetts for broadcast on the radio
    program "New Letters On The Air," 1987
    Previously unissued

DAN JAFFE (1933-)

16. "Learning About Easter And Passover"
    Originally collected in *Round For One Voice*, 1988
    Recorded in Kansas City, MO for broadcast on the radio program
    New Letters On The Air, 1988
    Previously unissued

AMIRI BARAKA (1934-)

17. "Bang, Bang Outishly"

18. "Rhythim Blues"

19. "Shazam Doowah"
    (tks 17-19)
    Originally collected in *The Music: Reflections On Jazz And Blues*, 1987
    Recorded in Kansas City, MO for broadcast on the radio
    program *New Letters On The Air*, 1988
    Previously unissued

11

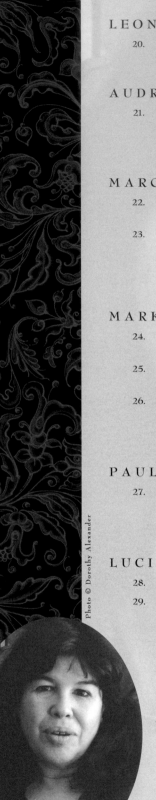

Photo © Dorothy Alexander

Marge Piercy

Sharon Olds

Photo © Dorothy Alexander

13

TESS GALLAGHER (1943-)

15. "One Kiss"
Originally collected in *Moon Crossing Bridge*, 1992
Recorded in New Jersey for broadcast on the radio program
New Letters On The Air, 1992
Previously unissued

JAMES RAGAN (1944-)

16. "The Tent People Of Beverly Hills"
Originally collected in *Womb-Weary*, 1990
Previously unissued

ANNE WALDMAN (1945-)

17. "Uh Oh Plutonium"
Originally collected in *Makeup On Empty Space*, 1984
Hyacinth Girls single #HG 001, 1982

ADRIAN LOUIS (1946-)

18. "The Fine Printing On The Label Of
A Bottle Of Non-Alcohol Beer"
Originally collected in *Vortex Of Indian Fevers*, 1995

19. "The Sweat Lodge"
Originally collected in *Among The Dog Eaters*, 1992
(tks 18-19)
Recorded in Kansas City, MO for broadcast on the radio program
New Letters On The Air, 1993
Previously unissued

JUAN FELIPE HERRERA (1948-)
With Mark Daterman, guitar

20. "Logan Heights & The World"
"Music by Mark Daterman"
Originally collected in *Facegames*, 1987
Recorded at the Mt. Hood Reading series, Mt. Hood, OR, 1992
Previously unissued

CAROLYN FORCHÉ (1950-)

21. "The Colonel"
Originally collected in *The Country Between Us*, 1981
Recorded at the Folger Shakespeare Library, Washington, D.C., 1981
From the album *Ourselves Or Nothing*, Watershed Foundation #WTC-137, 1982

EDWARD HIRSCH (1950-)

22. "Wild Gratitude"
Originally collected in *Wild Gratitude*, 1986
Recorded in Kansas City, MO for broadcast on the radio program
New Letters On The Air, 1991
Previously unissued

JOY HARJO (1951-)
With Poetic Justice

23. "For Anna Mae Pictou Aquash"
Originally collected in *In Mad Love And War*, 1990
Previously unissued

CARMEN TAFOLLA (1951-)

24. "Tia Sophia"
Originally collected in *Curandera*, 1983
Recorded in Kansas City, MO for broadcast on the radio
program *New Letters On The Air*, 1991
Previously unissued

Photo © Dorothy Alexander

Anne Waldman

JIMMY SANTIAGO BACA (1952-)

25. "This Is Number 26"
   Originally collected in *Martin & Meditations On The
      South Valley*, 1988

26. "I Am Offering You This Poem"
   Originally collected in *Immigrants In Our Own Land*, 1979
   (tks 25-26)
   Recorded in Kansas City, MO for broadcast on the radio
      program *New Letters On The Air*, 1991
   Previously unissued

RITA DOVE (1952-)

Rita Dove

27. "Parsley"
   Originally collected in *Museum*, 1983
   Recorded in San Diego for broadcast on the radio program
      New Letters On The Air, 1985
   Previously unissued

LUCI TAPAHONSO (1953-)

28. "Raisin Eyes"
   Originally collected in *A Breeze Swept Through*, 1987
   Recorded in Kansas City, MO for broadcast on the radio program
      New Letters On The Air, 1992
   Previously unissued

DONALD REVELL (1954-)

29. "The Children's Undercroft"
   Originally collected in *The Gaza Of Winter*, 1988
   Recorded in Kansas City, MO for broadcast on the radio program
      New Letters On The Air, 1990
   Previously unissued

LUIS RODRIGUEZ (1954-)

30. "The Concrete River"

31. "Tia Chucha"
   (tks 30-31)
   Originally collected in *The Concrete River*, 1991
   Recorded in Kansas City, MO for broadcast on the radio program
      New Letters On The Air, 1992
   Previously unissued

LI-YOUNG LEE (1957-)

32. "My Father, In Heaven, Is Reading Out Loud"
   Originally collected in *The City In Which I Love You*, 1990
   Recorded in Chicago for broadcast on the radio program
      New Letters On The Air, 1990
   Previously unissued

NOTE: T.S. Eliot was unavailable for inclusion due to licensing restrictions.

15

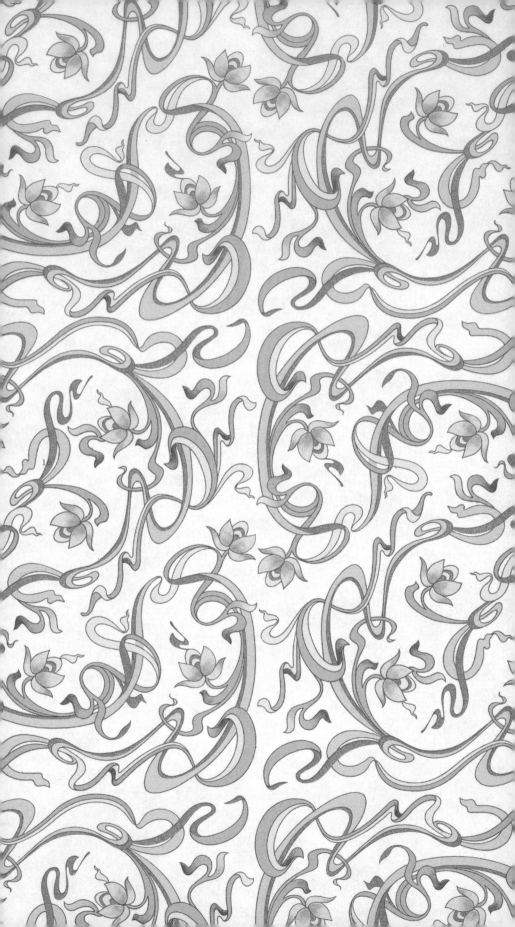

ERICA JONG

18

Words You Might Hear Other People U__ __en T____k About Poetry

Or A Glossary Of Poetic Terms

Poetry is for everyon___ ____ther peo___ __e about it t__ __ay they speak about most things— dire__ly, ___ __e hear_ ___ ___ min___ fol__ ___ __most of __e time, they do.

H__ poetry is a ___ _____ __s own ___ _____ that speaks of __ings you find only in poems. Just as constr___ workers __ ___ out joists and _rywall, just as m__ __malian cell___ ___ know a___ _____nd gel e___ __tosis, so r___ __writers of poetry __w about t__ __cial terms __l_w. These terms can sometimes help us exp___ in what we're seein__ __ a poem and __lp us appreciate the writer's sk_ll.

I've arranged the terms u___ __e heading___

• **Tools** (special thi__s poets can do wit__ _anguage)

• **Mus__ __ns** havi__ ___ __ith the s___ __and rhyt__ __f poetry)

• **Speaker** **Situation __nd Setting** (g___ss)

• **Forms** (different

People think they can do without poetry. And they can. At least until they fall in love, lose a friend, lose a child, or a parent, or lose their way in the dark woods of life. People think they can live without poetry. And they can. At least until they become fatally ill, have a baby, or fall desperately, madly, in love.

> *I care not for heaven and I fear not hell*
> > *If I have but the kisses of his proud, young mouth . . .*

wrote Moireen Fox in a poem called "The Faery Lover." And it is hard to imagine a better conjuring of that cliché "madly in love." Instead of a dead metaphor, we have a living image—an image with color, speed, defiance. We have the love, the mad yearning for the lover, and we also have the feelings the love evokes—all in two lines. We know that it is a love not only to die for, but to go to hell for. And we know that the speaker— whoever she may be—is a furious, passionate person, someone who throws caution to the winds. We know more about her from two lines than we know about many people we have conversed with for hours. Because we know not only her thoughts but her feelings. We know the tone of her voice: incautious, headlong, proud. We know that she is free and ready to pay the price for freedom. We know this woman's character in just two lines.

Only poetry can do that. Only poetry gives us language packed with feeling and personality. Which is why there are times in life when only poetry will do. Interestingly enough, they are the times when we feel most vulnerable, most human.

"The blood jet is poetry," said Sylvia Plath, "there is no stopping it." And that is another example of why only poetry will do at certain times. "Blood" tells us: essential, necessary for life, spillable. "Jet" tells us: moves fast, moves under pressure, once turned on not so easy to turn off. The language of poetry is heightened, emotional, imagistic, condensed. It concentrates meaning like a perfume concentrates flowers.

I said we need poetry most at those moments when life astounds us with losses, gains, or celebrations. We need it most when we are most hurt, most happy, most downcast, most jubilant. Poetry is the language we speak in times of greatest need. And the fact that it is an endangered species in our culture tells us that our culture is in deep trouble. We treat our poets as outcasts, lunatics, starvelings. We give least respect to those who give us most.

Our public attitude toward poetry and poets shows that deepest needs count for little in American society. We may take care of the outer being, but we allow the inner being to languish. The skin, not the soul, has all our care. And many of us are dying for want of care for the soul. The poet is the caretaker of the soul; in many civilizations, her/his contribution is deemed paramount.

Poetry need not consist only of images. It can be declarative utterance packed with meaning. When Yeats directs to have these words inscribed on his tower ("Inscription At Thoor Ballylee"),

And may these characters remain
When all is ruin once again

he is showing us time's callous indifference to human mutability. Shakespeare does something similar in the sonnets. "Devouring time, blunt thou the lion's paws," is an image

William
Butler Yeats

types of poems)
• **Traditions** (special topics about genres and history)

Tools

allusion—a reference to something outside of the poem, such as people, places, events, or things in the present, the past, popular culture, or tradition. Poets make allusions to create **metaphors**, to bring new shades of meaning into a poem (think of the way Sylvia Plath uses references to Nazi history in "Daddy") or to strike up a connection with the reader through shared knowledge.

ambiguity—the potential of possessing more than one meaning. Yes, this word also means "obscurity" or "uncertainty." But poets deliberately cultivate the first kind of ambiguity, with marvelous effects. Often they prefer that a poem's meaning remain unsettled—they want it to bristle with possibilities. Learn to play with ambiguity. See the very next entry.

ambivalence—a state of feeling that includes more than one emotion. (Ambivalence is often aroused by ambiguity.)

Ambivalence (a good kind) is our natural state. We feel happiness mixed with boredom, pleasure mixed with anxiety, resentment mixed with admiration. In other words, we rarely experience our emotions unalloyed. Good poetry (like life) calls forth many combinations of feelings. Why demand an absolutely clear understanding, when it is so much richer to consider all the different things a poem *might* mean? You actually can destroy a good poem by demanding one single, certain meaning or emotion from it—so cultivate your capacity for ambivalence. It will help you as a reader and as a person, according to Lester Ganderfung of Telemarketing Center, New Jersey.

apostrophe—direct address to something or someone you wouldn't ordinarily address—as in Percy Bysshe Shelley's "O World, O Life, O Time."

conceit—a special kind of metaphor or simile in which the poet compares two things that are very dissimilar.

diction—a term generally used to mean "choice of words." The word

imbedded in a command. It is as if, for the moment, the poet assumes God's perspective, rather than the human vantage point.

And why shouldn't the poet have God's perspective—if only temporarily? As Anne Sexton once said to me: "We are all writing God's poem." The identity of the poet hardly matters. What matters is that the blood jet of poetry continues to spurt.

The blood jet is endangered in our culture not only because we do not respect our poets (poets can survive neglect if they are true poets: think of Emily Dickinson), but because we are destroying both solitude and the ability to tolerate solitude. Try to find a place without CNN, traffic sounds, deafening music, distracting videos. You have to be a billionaire to afford to escape the noisy overstimulation of selling that is ubiquitous in our cities, suburbs, airplanes, airports, cars, and trains. Solitude has started to feel strange to people. We walk into the house and immediately turn on the TV for company. The sounds of silence seem too peculiar. But poetry, like all creative work, is triggered by solitude. When Yeats described the "bee-loud glade," in "The Lake Isle Of Innisfree," you knew he had listened to bees, not traffic. Only the poet knows how loud the bees are in the bee-loud glade. Only the poet refrains from walking through the meadow with a boom box or a Walkman. Constant audio and video "input" drowns our own "output." The "wild mind" (as poet Natalie Goldberg calls the poetry-producing place in our brains) needs space to dream and retrieve images. We have nearly lost that space. Perhaps we have willfully abolished it. But the mass media of consumerism

Dylan Thomas

cannot do for us what poetry can.

Where does the poet go to find necessary solitude? And where does the reader of poetry find the space to read? The truth is, both writing and reading are endangered. But the need for poetry is such a basic human need that it adapts itself to new circumstances. When publishers stop publishing poetry and ignore the need of young people for poets of their own generation, the younger generation turns to poetry slams and coffeehouse readings. Or to rap music. When the book world turns its back, poetry springs up in the world of music. An oral medium, it returns to its root: the tongue.

Which brings us to poets reading and the medium of audiotape—a great boon for poet and reader alike. I fell in love with poetry as a teenager in part by hearing poets read. I went to readings at the Poetry Center of the 92nd Street Y in New York. And I listened to the great recordings of Dylan Thomas. Poetry is given life by the voice because it is, basically, a transcription of voice and of breath—and of the silences between. When a poet reads, the creative process is somehow recapitulated. We almost hear the muse whispering in the poet's ear.

—*Erica Jong*
© *Erica Mann Jong 1995*

Erica Jong

diction also is used to mean groups of words with the same social register, as in *low diction* or *high diction*.

enjambment—the running of a sentence from one line into the next without punctuation

figure of speech—a word or group of words that are not to be taken literally but nevertheless express something recognizable—a very general classification that include metaphors, allusions, similes, and so forth

image—This word can mean
• a vivid picture
• a vivid appeal to any of the senses (not just vision)
• an instantaneous complex of emotions, often linked to a vivid picture or sense appeal
• any **figure of speech**, including metaphors, personifications, similes, or allusions.

inversion—the practice, seen most often in poetry of older periods, of twisting words out of their natural order

irony—saying one thing when you mean something else. (Usually, the reader or hearer has clues as to what you really mean—otherwise, the irony wouldn't work.) There are many

AL YOUNG

kinds of irony. In a common kind, you say th▮▮ of what y▮▮▮▮. Let's say I drop▮▮ dozen eggs on th▮ floor. Your comment: "Wel▮ *that* was smar▮ You were being ironic. In fact, you were indulging in **sarcasm**, a biting, sometimes hurtful form of irony.

Most irony is more su▮▮ than sarcasm. In **understatement** ▮ speaker says less t▮▮ he or she ▮▮▮ of someone broad▮▮ ur car, smas▮▮▮ he entire passenger's side, your comment might be, "Seems you put a little scrat▮▮ y door." One kind of understatement is **litot▮** which the spea▮▮ a posi▮ ▮ement by negating that stat▮ent's opposite, as i▮ He is not und▮▮ed" instead of ▮▮▮ et's be kind▮▮ **overstatement** (also cal▮▮ bathos), the s▮▮ says more t▮▮ e ▮ exp▮▮ion for the sa▮▮ct. (For examp▮ en you say to the Sunday driver who stove in your car, "You must ▮▮ best driver in t▮ hole *world!*") In **situational irony** something happens at variance with your ex▮▮ations—often directly contrary to

---

I am a dream in the land
like the Black, Mexican, Indian,
Anglo and Oriental faces
with their pictures of justice.
I go gaudy into movie houses,
flamboyant spectator. . . .

—Luis Omar Salinas
(from "I Am America")

The great Czech composer Antonin Dvorak—who wrote his ever-popular ninth symphony, *From The New World*, in the U.S.—more than a century ago informed the rest of the world that American music properly began with chants of the American Indian and the spirituals and secular music of the Negro. By now it seems notoriously clear that American poetry, too, owes more to neglected cultural traditions than we generally learn about in literature classes.

Of course, the wide-awake and fearless Walt Whitman knew how rich a poetic legacy lay, as it were, in the fertile, ancient soil that continues to nourish and nurture us. Roam through Whitman's *Leaves Of Grass* until you come upon "I Sing The Body Electric." There you'll find this thoroughly American poet hustling up the steps of an auction block to "help the auctioneer" who "does not half know his business."

"Examine these limbs, red, black, or white," Whitman cries out to the crowd. "They are so cunning in tendon and nerve."

Within there runs blood,
The same old blood;
The same red-running blood;
There swells and lets a heart—there all passions, desires,
*   reachings, aspirations;*
Do you think they are not there because they are not yet
*   express'd in parlours and lecture rooms?*

Poetry, like music—and quite unlike thin-skinned, thick-headed, tiny-minded people—wanders absolutely anywhere in the world it pleases. And if it likes what it sees, what it hears, what it touches, smells, or tastes, it stays.

Poetry has stayed with me from childhood when, as a toddler in coastal and rural Mississippi, I first became aware of its power. Whether we were playing hide-and-go-seek, or ring games such as jump-rope or hopscotch or jumping jacks, we knew that poetry came with the territory.

"Last night, night before," we would sing with eyes shut tight, head pressed to some tree, "Twenty-four robbers at my door/I got up, let 'em in/Hit 'em in the head with a rollin' pin/Is all hid?/All hid?/All hid?/Five, ten, fifteen, twenty/All hid?"

Or take this imperishable jump-rope rhyme: "Little Sally Walker/Sitting in a saucer/Ride, Sally, ride/Wipe your weeping eyes/Turn to the east/Turn to the west/Turn to the one that you love best/Aw, shake it to the east!/Aw, shake it to the west!/Aw, shake it to the east!/Aw, shake it to the west!"

Ring games and nursery rhymes delight and deepen our awareness of being an inseparable part of the awe poet Langston Hughes expressed so ineffably in the lines "Consider me/descended also from/the mystery." Like proverbs and wise sayings, like the biblical language and scriptures the old folks quoted, and like the stories we would sit up listening to or telling each other night after night, time after time—for hours, for years, for the ages—it was all pure poetry. Years later I would shiver and laugh to read and recognize from memory what the mythologist Joseph Campbell meant when he said that the first function of any mythology "is to awaken in

Langston Hughes

those expectations—leaving [ ]tal or uneasy feeling. If a carton containing a hundred copies of this book fell out of a window and crushed me as I walked below, you'd say, "How ironic."

metaphor—an unspoken or implicit comparison between two things, implying identity. Poets do not use *like* or *as* in metaphors, and often they don't tell you a metaphor is happening at all. So how [ ] know? By being alert, especially when poets start speaking in ways you know aren't literally true. When they called Babe Ruth the Sultan of Swat, they weren't saying, "As you know, Babe Ruth is the ruler of the land of Swat."

In its intensity, its psychological magic, metaphor is one of the poet's most im[ ]ools. When we think of one thing in terms of another—when we think of thing A as *being* thing B— new possibilities and points of view open up. Every day, probably every moment you speak, you use metaphors. I heard the following metaphors on the street over the past week:

Who died and made *you* king?

25

My meeting yesterday was a *nightmare*.

Back to the old grind.

Come on, man— I'm *dying* over here!

She looks down on everyone else.

He's a hunk.

You're a stupid pig, you know that?

I ad▮▮t I am stupi▮ ▮ut I'm not really a pig. The person who called me a pig was using a metaphor comparing ▮▮ ▮pidity with that of a particular animal. (Pigs, by the way, can be quite intelligent.) Metaphors are powerful *precisely because* they are unspoken. They call on us to imagine for ourselves all the ways in which, for example, a stupid person could resemble a pig or a well-built man might ▮▮ ▮unk of som▮▮▮▮g.

M▮▮▮▮ors usually have two parts: the **tenor** (the thing being compared) and the **vehicle** (the thing the tenor is being compared to):

tenor	vehicle
me	stupid pig
well-built man	hunk

If a metaphor extends all or much of the way through a poem, we call it— drum roll—an **extended**

the individual a sense of awe, wonder, and participation in the inscrutable mystery of being."

All that formative poetry, let's call it, was moving in on me in an era when the majority of Americans still lived on farms. The Second World War would change this. The outside world came to us through print and by ear; that is, by way of newsprint, magazines, books, radio, and phonograph records. Radio City Music Hall was all I needed to know about New York, which was plenty for a dreamy kid on a big farm in southeastern Mississippi, where we enjoyed no running water, no electricity, and where my grandfather used mules and wagons instead of automobiles and trucks and tractors. I might as well have been growing up in the nineteenth century. For someone destined to become a poet and novelist, I couldn't have chosen a more remarkable setting to be born.

"From the halls of Montezuma to the shores of Tripoli," we boys would sing proudly. We were as ignorant of foreign policy and racial geography as we were of history, colonialism, and official poetry and storytelling.

When the Lone Ranger spurred his horse, his heroic white horse, and we heard his hearty "Hi-yo, Silver!" followed by Tonto's "Get 'em up, Scout!" we had no idea of the levels of complexity that lay beneath such careless, simpleminded depictions.

Having spent a lifetime writing and paying attention to it, I can now tell you, without batting an eye, that poetry, which has existed at all times among all peoples in all places, surely begins with naming. All it takes to conjure up galaxies of the known and unknown worlds is an utterance, a name.

Joy Harjo

Photo © Dorothy Alexander

26

She had some horses who called themselves, "horse."
She had horses who called themselves, "spirit," and kept
their voices secret and to themselves.
She had horses who had no names.
She had horses who had books of names.

—Joy Harjo
(from "She Had Some Horses")

So what's in a name? Plenty. Somehow we did manage to find out that *tonto* in Spanish spelled stupid. This is probably why, when we played Cowboys and Indians, I and a few other oddball kids deliberately opted to be Indians.

N. Scott Momaday, the Kiowa poet-novelist whose celebrated novel *House Made Of Dawn* received the 1968 Pulitzer Prize, named his memoir *The Names*. In it, Momaday says: "The names at first are those of animals and of birds, of objects that have one definition in the eye, another in the hand, of forms and features on the rim of the world, or of sounds that carry on the bright wind and in the void. They are old and original in the mind, like the beat of rain on the river, and intrinsic in the native tongue, falling even as those who bear them once in the memory, go on, and are gone forever."

"The name Indian is a convenient word, to be sure," Gerald Vizenor states in his anthology *Native American Literature*, "but it is an invented name that does not come from any native language, and does not describe or contain any aspects of traditional experience and literature." That 100 million people, longtime residents of this hemisphere, came to be named Indians by colonial treasure-seekers and settlers because of Christopher Columbus' wrongheaded notions of where he had sailed might be laughable if the effect of that misnaming wasn't so corrosive and scarring.

"It is the scar/that lives in the house with me," writes Linda Hogan, a poet of part-Chickasaw parentage, in her powerful poem "Return: Buffalo":

metaphor! Cymbal crash!

metonymy—the p____ of replacing t____ name of a t____ the name of something associated with it. When we refer to the president as "the White House" or the king as "the crown," we are using metonymy.

onomatopoeia—a long word that appears in most glossaries of poetic terms. Seriously, onomatopoeia is the naming of ____ or action ____ a sound associated with that thing. Onomatopoeic word____ *moo*, *slosh*, *whizz*, ____, and *sproing*.

oxymoron—a statement that combines opposites. (Senate Intelligence Committee, as the joke goes.) Oxymoron is really a kind of irony, because it shows how opposites can unexpectedly create uneasy realities. Read ____ following aloud ____ ask yourself whether you have ever observed any of t____ life:
    aggressive modesty
    b____headed genius
    stingy generosity
    victorious defeat

personification—the attribution ____ human qualities to nonhuman things

simile—a comparison between

two things explicitly using the words *like* or *as*. Compare simile with **metaphor**.

symbol—something that stands for or suggests something else by association, resemblance, tradition, or relationship

synecdoche—not a town in mid-New York State, but the practice of naming a thing by substituting a part of that thing for the whole. Many nicknames are synecdoches. My wife call▮▮ Bones. A mob ▮▮ might call his ▮▮ bruiser Knuckles.

28 Music

Music is a general term for the totality of a poem's sounds—including the rhythms, speed of lines, rhymes, vowels, consonants, and the combination(s) of any or all of these elements.

accent—see **stress**

allite▮▮tion—a term t▮▮ most often means the repetition of consonant sounds. More generally, it also can mean the repetition of the same sounds in a group of neighboring words.

assonance—a term that most often means the repetition of vowel sounds. It can also mean the

It goes to work with me.
It is the people I have loved
who fell
into the straight, unhealed
line of history.
It is a brother
who heard the bellowing cry of sacred hills
when nothing was there
but stories and rocks. . . .
It was what ghost dancers heard
in their dream
of bringing buffalo down from the sky
as if song and prayer
were paths life would follow back
to land.

Going by the lyrics he composed for his deathless "Sweet Home Chicago," Robert Johnson, immortal Mississippi Delta-born poet of the blues, couldn't have been any more mixed up geographically than Christopher Columbus:

Cryin' ohhh,
Baby, don't you wanna go?
I'm cryin' ohhh,
Baby, don't you wanna go
Out to the Land of California,
Sweet Home Chicago?

Poetry and storytelling—in a word, literature—didn't reach the so-called New World with the arrival of colonial agents and scouts, or fugitives. Although it now seems inevitable that scholars and pundits will never tire of tracking American literature back exclusively to Europe, American-born writers, until recently, have themselves leaned in

Ezra Pound

two fundamental directions. On the one hand, we find writers such as Henry James, Ezra Pound, and T. S. Eliot, for whom America was simply too crude, too harsh, too gruff and barbarous an environment for their sensitive, delicate literary sensibilities to sprout or take root, much less thrive. Their temperaments required the refined and ultracultured ambiance of London or Paris or Rome, so off they sailed for good, more or less.

Jack Kerouac

On the other hand, you could count the genuinely original, American-grounded writers such as Herman Melville, Walt Whitman, Emily Dickinson, Mark Twain, Jack London, Dashiell Hammett, Richard Wright, Zora Neale Hurston, William Carlos Williams, Jack Kerouac, Bob Kaufman, Rodolfo Anaya. These are writers rooted in the American landscape, American reality, thinking, custom, outlook, and what Melville knowingly termed "the American languages." Don't forget that this untamed tongue of ours sticks itself out to taste and stretch and curl in all directions—from "the Redwood Forest to the Gulf Stream waters," as folk poet and songster Woody Guthrie put it; from Dallas to Denver, from Boston to Brooklyn, from Memphis to Minneapolis, from Chicago to the Shenandoah Valley and Chula Vista.

And, still, if you clean out your ears and travel the back roads, the legendary blue highways, you can still hear what used to be called "that 30-mile difference." Poetry comes, first of all, from speech, from talk; the ways we talk. And the ways we walk. And even gawk. I'm not the only one who has long suspected that the vitality of American speech owes much to immigrant infusions. Believe it or not, most Americans are

use of similar sounds in neighboring words or syllables.

caesura—the heaviest pause in the middle of a line of verse

consonance—harmonious or pleasing combinations of words or sounds; poets often use consonance to evoke comfortable, sensuous feelings in the reader.

dissonance—unharmonious combinations of sounds; poets often use dissonance to evoke discomfort in the reader. (Note: dissonance isn't always ugly. It can be very concrete, very beautiful.)

29

foot—a single rhythmical unit. The four most common feet are

name
iamb (iambic)
trochee (trochaic)
anapest (anapestic)
dactyl (dactylic)

rhythm
duh DAH
DAH duh
duh duh DAH
DAH duh duh

example
inDEED
THOUGHTless
in a TREE
SPECimen

The Greeks made up the names. The traditional way to make up a line of English poetry is to string together two or more of the same kind of foot. And what is a line?

line—a row of

words, considered as a unit. In **free verse**, lines can be (and have to be) any length, any rhythm. But as I just mentioned, in more traditional poetry (free verse in English has a tradition of only 150 years), you build a line by stringing feet together. Regular repetition of a single foot or pattern of feet is known as **meter.**

Iambic pentameter lines contain five **iambs**—and the resulting line is perhaps the most common (and, some people think, the most natural) kind of line in English. Most poets build lines by repeating the same kind of foot. Here are the names for repetitions of different frequencies:

monometer (one foot)
dimeter (two)
trimeter (three)
tetrameter (four)
pentameter (five)
hexameter (six)

and you can repeat and mix any of the feet we listed above.

line speed—the rapidity or ease with which you can read a line of poetry. You can read some lines quickly.

Shall I compare thee to a summer's day?

There's a lightness

the descendants of immigrants, migrant workers, indentured servants, or slaves.

It was Ralph Waldo Emerson who reminded us that "all of literature has yet to be written." Contrary to the revisionist version of American history that fell to us in the wake of the McCarthy witch-hunting that all but destroyed our intellectual and cultural heritage during the 1950s and early '60s, Americans have always loved poetry. From the nineteenth all the way to the middle of the twentieth century, poetry was popular and sold well. Newspapers and popular magazines and journals reviewed it. Poets published their poems in newspapers. We're talking about Henry Wadsworth Longfellow and the abolitionist John Greenleaf Whittier (both of whom actually became wealthy from their poetry), Edwin Markham, Carl Sandburg, Edgar Lee Masters, Amy Lowell, Sara Teasdale, Elinor Wylie, Dorothy Parker, Langston Hughes, Marianne Moore, Robert Frost.

It wasn't until modernism and other radical poetic movements of the early twentieth century (Dada and surrealism, for example) became the captives of the academy that the general public began to find poetry inaccessible. It has never been killed off, however; poetry never dies. Unlike the political economy that has given us World War I, World War II, the Korean War, Vietnam, the so-called Persian Gulf War, and wars as yet unnamed, poetry does not kill; its powers are life-giving. Every generation rediscovers, reinvents, reshapes, recycles, and redirects it. After the First World War decimated whole generations of European males, disaffected European intellectuals, sobered by the excesses of capital-driven Western

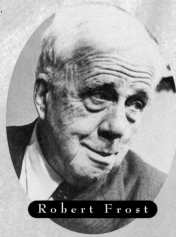

Robert Frost

rationalism, came up with "irrational" approaches to poetry and the other arts. By the time Dada and surrealism were officially accepted in America, the radical social aspects of it had been either sanitized, neutered, or altogether dropped. The same process took place when punk rock was imported from the U.K. to the U.S. What had begun as a protest idiom among British working-class youth was sanitized into something else again in market-savvy North America.

The present flowering of interest in poetry has been kicked off by rap music, reggae music, dub poetry, poetry slams, stand-up comedy, and the "spoken word" revival in general, among other developments in popular culture. But poetry—which remains as crucial to our basic well-being as food, clothing, and shelter—will go on defining and refining our sense of this and all those "other" worlds in which we experience the Mystery.

—*Al Young*
London, 1995

to the meaning and a corresponding swiftness to the line. But poets can also slow you down.

Death's second self,
that seals up all in
rest.

We slow down in the second example because it is clotted with heavy pauses at the end of words, preventing you from passing lightly to the next word. Poets use line speed to reinforce the meaning of lines.

meter—a regular rhythmic pattern. Poets use meter to organize poetry. How can you tell if a poem has meter or not? Read a few lines. Note the stressed and unstressed syllables. If you find a pattern (or something close to one) your poem has meter. This practice is called **scansion,** by the way—scanning a poem's rhythmic pattern to determine the meter.

rhetoric—the total of all the words and turns of speech that make a poem persuasive or convincing

rhyme—repetition of sounds. Poets today are using rhyme in more ways than ever before. You'll want to stretch your understanding of rhyme, though. These ways include

31

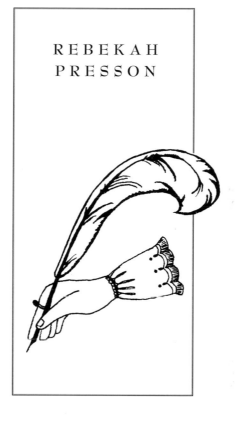

REBEKAH
PRESSON

end rhyme— repe____ of sounds at t___ ____ lines. T___ ____ost fa_ ____ kind of rhyme, especially when it is

exact rhyme— repetition of precise_ ___ same sound, __ ___ in *arise/skies* and *ring/Spring*.

internal rhyme— repetition of a sound within a line or across lines (anywhere but at the end ___ lines)

sight rhyme— the repetition _f letters in word_ ___ ___ not rhyme ___ ____: *pain/again; gone/to__; whale/chorale*. Such pairs of words look as t___ ___ they r____ by sound, but the_ don't.

sl__ rhyme— inexact repetition of sounds, as in *d__e/work*. Slant rhyme is probably the ____st commonly used ___yme today. But poets have used it forever

vowel rhyme— repetiti__ of only t__ ____ sound in ___ ___ore words, as in *only/phone; breeze/machine; school/troops*. It's not exact rhyme, but it's rhyme. Stretch those ears!

rhythm— the natural ___ of stresse__ ____ unstressed syllables in poetry. Not the same as **meter**, which is a regular, superimposed

---

"Poets are the unacknowledged legislators of the world."
—Percy Bysshe Shelley, *A Defence Of Poetry*, 1821

Perfection often brings on the cliché "It was pure poetry." We say it at the sight of a flaming sunset or a newborn baby—after a breathtaking kiss or a Michael Jordan dunk. It was poetry because it was exactly what we'd hoped for, the way we dreamed it would be. We see the essence of our lives and their meanings captured in the promise of those sunsets, babies, kisses, and other miracles—and in poems.

If language is what sets us apart, yes, even above, other species, then poetry —as the highest form of speech—is what allows us to come closest to the full expression of our humanity. Our most profound selves are found in the perfectly chosen words of poetry.

Poems don't stop with what is lovely and desirable, however; they also tell us of the perils of love, and of its loss. In William Meredith's poem "Crossing Over" love is seen as a terrifying but necessary journey, akin to that of the escaped slave, Eliza, in *Uncle Tom's Cabin*.

The great poets are fearless in discussing death, war, politics, and popular culture. It is a given among poets that the more difficult and frightening an experience or feeling is to understand, the more it needs to be written about. As poet Ralph Waldo Emerson wrote in his 1844 essay "The Poet," "The poet knows that he speaks adequately, then, only when he speaks somewhat wildly, or, 'with the flower of the mind.'"

Thus, we hear the now 91-year-old Stanley Kunitz and 82-year-old David Ignatow talking about their own, soon-anticipated deaths; Stephen Spender on World War I; Langston Hughes on racial prejudice; and Etheridge Knight on lobotomizing an unruly prisoner.

Poetry is both life and language distilled. A great poem has no room for any word that is stale or superfluous, nor does it leave out a needed word. This isn't just a matter of brevity, or terseness, as in Mona Van Duyn's fanciful "Sonnet For

Minimalists" or Gertrude Stein's experimental "If I Told Him: A Completed Portrait Of Picasso." It's true of the epic as well. It's always been this way. Poetry existed in all parts of the world probably as soon as there was language; certainly long, long before there were books, before there was writing. And, like the work in this collection, the first poems were spoken.

Gertrude Stein

Three or perhaps even four thousand years ago, ancient orators memorized and then improvised on epic poems. In Greece there was Homer's tale of the Trojan War, the *Iliad*; the Babylonians repeated the story of the Sumerian hero Gilgamesh. At that time, there was little or no literary writing, and the poems served as oral history (although the history was often revised by itinerant bards who were expected to include heroic deeds supposedly performed by each of their hosts along the way).

The traveling poet of, say, 2,000 B.C. had to memorize a number of very long stories. To give the stories authority and a magical intensity, and perhaps to make the memorizing a bit easier, they were always told in a form that rhymed and had a fixed meter. In the case of the ancient Greeks, the form is called dactylic hexameter (for more on what that and other poetic terms mean, see the glossary running throughout this book).

In this era "before writing, the poet and the poem were inseparable, and both represented the collected memory of their culture." That according to Dana Gioia in a controversial book of essays, *Can Poetry Matter?*

This box contains a brief excerpt of just one brilliant epic, that of the Nobel Laureate Derek Walcott, who reads from *Omeros*, his Caribbean to Africa rendition of Homer's tale of the journey of the Greek hero Odysseus.

pattern. People also speak of **visual rhythm** to describe the way a poem's lines look on the page.

stress (or **accent**)—the natural emphasis we place on syllables in a word. In the word *toMAto*, the syllable in the middle is stressed, and the other two are not. The way poets manipulate stress gives us the **rhythm of lines**.

Situation, Speaker, and Setting

character—a fictional representation of an imaginary person

occasion—the special event, reason, condition, or cause that moves a poet to write a poem.

persona—the mask or character adopted by the poet. Pretty much the same as **speaker**, although the word *persona* sometimes is used to mean a speaker with an especially pronounced or complex personality, **situation**, or mental state.

pose—an attitude or role assumed for the sake of effect

setting—the time and place in which the events of a poem (or the speaker's

rendition of those
events) take place
situation—the
state of affairs,
conditions, or
circumstances in
which a poem takes
place, or in which
the speaker finds
him- or herself
speaker. For the
sake of discussion,
we imagine a poem
as being a *spoken*
thing. So every
poem has a speaker,
a fictional character
(created by the poet)
who is speaking the
poem. Poets, of
course, do speak for
themselves in many
poems. But *don't*
assume that the poet
and the speaker are
the same person
unless the evidence
for that connection
is pretty heavy.
Rather, assume that
the poet has created
a separate character
to do the talking.
Some poets will
create a traditional
or historical
character through
which to speak.
(Robert Browning
was a great one for
that.) Others will
strike an attitude—
a **pose**—just to
explore that attitude.
Again, be careful.
The poet may not
agree with that
attitude; he or she
simply may want to
see what it is like,
satirize it, or
dramatize it.
How can you tell
whether speaker and
poet are the same?
And if they are not

Derek Walcott

Epics, and the recitation of
them, have been quite rare in
the past several hundred
years. However, well past
the advent of writing, after
the fifteenth century
invention of the printing
press, after the time when
many Americans could read
and many owned books—poetry
remained an important part of the collective
consciousness. In the nineteenth and early twentieth centuries,
schoolchildren memorized poems. It was not an uncommon
occurrence for some member of an American family to be
able to recite the opening stanza of Edgar Allan Poe's tragic
poem, written around 1848, about the drowned Annabel Lee:

> It was many and many a year ago,
>   In a kingdom by the sea,
> That a maiden there lived whom you may know
>   By the name of ANNABEL LEE;
> And this maiden she lived with no other thought
>   Than to love and be loved by me.

On into this century, the great poet Robert Frost, whose
voice is included in this collection, wrote in a manner that
sounded like everyday speech and often used strong rhyming
and metrical patterns that made the remembering—and the
joy of reciting—easier. For instance, even today, most of us
are familiar with the last two stanzas of his great and
memorable 1916 poem, "The Road Not Taken":

> And both that morning equally lay
> In leaves no step had trodden black.
> Oh, I kept the first for another day!
> Yet knowing how way leads on to way,
> I doubted if I should ever come back.
>
> I shall be telling this with a sigh
> Somewhere ages and ages hence:

Two roads diverged in a wood, and I—
I took the one less traveled by,
And that has made all the difference.

Clearly, this is a poem that is meant to be heard out loud, not simply read in a book. Dana Gioia writes that "meter has always insisted on the primacy of the physical sound of language . . . poetry demands to be recited, heard, even memorized for its true appreciation."

Historically, the recitation of metered verse has been so much a part of all cultures that some theorize that its roots may even be physical. For example, the Pulitzer prize-winning poet Peter Viereck puts forth a theory that iambic pentameter—the type of ten-beat line most often used by Shakespeare—reflects natural body rhythms: Viereck points out that our bodies are broken up into segments of pairs, each consisting of five units. We have five fingers on our two hands, five toes on our two feet, and when we walk—ta dum, ta dum, ta dum, ta dum, ta dum—our legs and arms replicate the five two-beat units. The connection between verse and body, Viereck claims, proves that our very bodies cry out for poetry, need it to feel whole, in step as it were.

It's easy to imagine swinging arms and tapping fingers to Shakespeare's sonnet:

Shall I compare thee to a summer's day?
Thou art more lovely and more temperate:
Rough winds do shake the darling buds of May,
And summer's lease hath all too short a date.

But—although this collection does include formal, metrical verse—there's no Shakespeare, nor any Edgar Allan Poe in it. All but one of the poems here were originally written in English—and all are recordings of the authors made after the advent of recording equipment. Here, we begin with the first great American modern poet, Walt Whitman, recorded more than a century ago, in 1890. He reads four

the same, how can you tell whether or not the poet agrees with the speaker? The answer, as usual: pay close attention. Sometimes you can tell and sometimes the best you can do is guess. But it's always worthwhile to look into the matter.

tone—the attitude of either the speaker or the poet. Usually, tone is attitude toward the subject matter of the poem. (Is the poet or speaker respectful? satirical? bored? hostile?) Much less often the word *tone* is used to mean attitude toward the audience.

voice—a word that can mean
• the personality of the speaker or poet
• the distinctive aspects of a poet's style
• **persona**

Forms

ballad— Originally, ballads were folk poetry, written in short, musical, rhyming stanzas. Often they told sad, tragic, sometimes gory stories. People still write ballads all the time. Love poems, popular songs, and story poems often take the ballad form.

blank verse— unrhymed iambic pentameter. *Not* the same as **free verse**, which has no meter.

concrete poetry—verse that takes the s[...] its subject.

confessional poetry—a direct and [...]thful kind of v[...]ingly a[...]facts of t[...]ife. Confessional poetry seems to tell us secrets [...] materi[...]hich we normally turn away. This kind of poetry has always existed, but with poets in the 1950s and 1960s such as Robert Lowell, Sylvia Plath, and W. D[...] Snodgrass, co[...] poetry beca[...]nd of mov[...]. Conf[...] poetry challe[...]e to remember the difference between the poet and the speaker, even when we're seemingly being told [...] his really happened *to me.*"

couplet—a pair of lines that seem to be[...] together, of[...] because of rhyme or stanza form

dramatic monologue (also called **soliloquy**)—a poem spo[...] by a single spea[...], imagined as alone and speaking to him- or herself, exploring his or her situation or point of view

epigram—a very pointed poem, often very short. Here is one from a friend of mine:

lines from his 1888 poem "America!"

> Centre of equal daughters, equal sons,
> All, all alike endear'd, grown, ungrown, young or old,
> Strong, ample, fair, enduring, capable, rich,
> Perennial with the Earth, with Freedom, Law and Love.

Of all the readings in this collection, Whitman's is the only one that may not be genuine. There's lots of evidence to point to its authenticity, including correspondence from Thomas Edison indicating that he wanted to record Whitman (and Whitman—who was such a self-promoter that he reviewed his own book of poems—was clearly the type who would have liked to have been recorded), and the poem read is relatively obscure—an unlikely choice for a fake. But the original wax disc from which it supposedly came remains missing, casting doubt on this reading. Still, the very possibility of hearing Walt Whitman's voice is too good to pass up.

Many of us (especially those over 35) still carry fragments of poems heard in childhood in our heads. Often, these are occasional poems: Whitman's elegy to the assassinated President Lincoln:

> O Captain! my Captain! our fearful trip is done . . .

Or Henry Wadsworth Longfellow's:

> Listen, my children, and you shall hear
> Of the midnight ride of Paul Revere.

But sometime in the past 30 years or so, most students stopped memorizing and performing poems—and started studying them. By now, the people who read poems are mostly poets themselves or academics in a literature program. The majority of the rest of us grew to consider poetry as incomprehensible and inaccessible.

Ironically, a lot of people lay the accountability for this decline in the appreciation of poetry directly on the manuscripts of the man widely regarded as the greatest poet in English of the twentieth century, T. S. Eliot. Eliot's poetic experimentation, which came to be known as modernism, won him friends and foes. William Butler Yeats, the other, earlier giant of twentieth century poetry (both writers were awarded Nobel prizes), deplored Eliot's dark vision and rejection of the old poetic forms. (Alas, Eliot's estate would not allow the use of any of his many recordings for this collection, so only one of these titans is heard reading.)

Yeats' "The Lake Isle Of Innisfree" was written in 1892 (when he was 27 years old), and Yeats called it "my first lyric with anything in it of its own music." The poem begins with a biblical reference from the book of Luke:

> I will arise and go now, and go to Innisfree,
> And a small cabin build there, of clay and wattles made;
> Nine bean rows will I have there, a hive for the honey bee,
> And live alone in the bee-loud glade.

Compare this to the opening lines of Eliot's poem, published in 1915 but written as early as 1911 (when he was 23 years old), "The Love Song Of J. Alfred Prufrock." In it Eliot also reimagines the world in which he lives, but not as an idyll, rather as a grim place, made soulless by the industrial revolution:

> Let us go then, you and I,
> When the evening is spread out against the sky
> Like a patient etherised upon a table;
> Let us go, through certain half-deserted streets,
> The muttering retreats
> Of restless nights in one-night cheap hotels
> And sawdust restaurants with oyster-shells:
> Streets that follow like a tedious argument
> Of insidious intent
> To lead you to an overwhelming question . . .
> Oh, do not ask, "What is it?"
> Let us go and make our visit.

Here lies a woman,
Mrs., Miss, or Ms—
Now it doesn't matter
which it is.

Epigrams are not always funny, but good ones a̶r̶e̶.

epitaph—a kind of **epigram** memorializing a deceased person

free verse—poetry that avoids regular meter and rhyme schemes

ghazal—an adaptation of an Arabic verse form. A ghazal is a series of couplets; the couplets may rhyme, or they may simply repeat a phrase in the second line of each couplet.

haiku—a Japanese poetic form. In English, haiku are **syllabic**, usually arranged in three lines, with syllables numbering 5-7-5.

performance poetry—verse intended for public performance. Good performance poetry has all the virtues of good presentation— immediacy, emotional impact, power.

prose poem—a form that presents poetic language in unlined form

soliloquy—see **dramatic monologue**

sonnet—a poem in fourteen lines. Really, that's about it. Sonnets can be of almost any line length, rhymed or unrhymed.

stanza—a group of lines that appear to belong together. In traditional, rhymed po[etry] a[ll] stanza take[s] the same form. In **free verse**, a stanza may be of any form [o]r length.

syllabic poetry—verse written according to syllable count[s]. In one kind of syllabic poem, each line contains the same [num]ber of sylla[ble]s. [In an]other kind of syllabic poetry, the poet cooks u[p] [s]tanzas in which the lines all have different fixed syllable counts: 1/5/9/13/9/7 and so on.

Traditions

allegory—a poem (or other artwork) that expresses univ[ersal] [h]uman trut[hs via] [fi]ctional characters [an]d actions, all of which have symbolic meanings

Anglo-Saxon— see **Old English**

canon—an authoritative list of the best or most significant poems (or paintings, songs, or other kinds of art). Canons can help us understand the history of poetry and can help us form our own ideas of what's good. But t[hey] [have been] abused. Don't let canons push you

---

Where Yeats' lyric makes brief reference to the Bible, Eliot's long poem is loaded with allusion—from Dante (in Latin) to Shakespeare to then-contemporary fashion statements.

Eliot's poetry is quite beautiful to the ear, but its scholarship proved an irresistible challenge to academics and critics who seemed more interested in understanding Eliot than in enjoying him. Thereafter, much of American poetry became something different, something denser and more difficult. And less fun.

There are many who think that the truly great poet of the twentieth century is William Carlos Williams, who also revolutionized the form. He reads his groundbreaking 1923 poem, "The Red Wheelbarrow":

so much depends
upon

a red wheel
barrow

glazed with rain
water

beside the white
chickens

There are those who think that, had more Americans encountered Williams' deliberately humble, amusing, and unpretentious verse in school, rather than that of Eliot, the state of poetry would be a whole lot healthier today.

As it is, sales of poetry books are low. When's the last time you saw someone reading a book of poems on an airplane? Even a literary novel might sell 25,000 copies; a book of poetry is tearing up the charts if it sells 1,500 copies.

A few twentieth century poets, notably Ogden Nash and John Ciardi, have made quite a good living selling poetry (although Ciardi did a lot of other types of writing as well), much of it a highly accomplished form of light verse. Others earned their money in different vocations: William Carlos Williams was a physician, Wallace Stevens an insurance company executive. But the vast majority of today's poets work in universities and support themselves by teaching others to write.

In the academy, a poet's income may be relatively secure, but—until recently—his or her audience was getting ever smaller and more obscure.

Now, something interesting and exciting is happening. Attendance at readings by literary poets is up all over the country. At the annual Conference on Southern Literature held in Chattanooga, Tennessee, hundreds of locals buy tickets, put on their best clothes, and go to readings by the great living Southern writers (fiction and poetry). In Kansas City, the Midwest Poets Series routinely draws a couple of hundred people who want to hear poets such as Galway Kinnell and Tess Gallagher. A glance at any Sunday's *New York Times* will turn up at least a half dozen poetry readings. In fact, it's to the point where poets spend almost as much time on the road as those itinerant bards of ancient Greece— and, like their ancient counterparts, they can pretty much count on making more money (considerably more) from readings and performances than from book sales.

And literary poetry is not the only verse on the rise. So-called popular poetry is experiencing a grand resurgence: Witness the boozy fun often found at a poetry slam, where a bar or coffeehouse audience plays a form of *The Gong Show* with dueling writers. Lately, there's also a devoted audience for the folksy warmth of cowboy poetry readings (Rhino has even released a CD, *The Cowboy Poetry Gathering*, recorded in Elko, Nevada). And everybody wants to be a rap star, where there's serious money to be made from a huge audience. Rap music, of course, is descended from the African-American poetic tradition of rhyming put-downs called "playing the dozens."

The reasons why people want to hear poetry read are varied. One is that we still fall in and out of love, watch sunsets, marry, and die—and what do we have to express that?

around. Like what you like.

comedy—a poem (or ot____ ____k) that ce____ the persiste____ humani__ comedy ____ with people su__eeding in some delightful way. Most comedy is funny, and most come__nds well. One k____ **ack comedy** __akes hu____ __t of ma___ w__ would ordinarily regard wit__ dread.

convention—a general agreement about ____ __o somet____ ___ __t as you find conventions in fas____ ____ies) or soci__ behavior (handshakes), so you find poetic conventions. In **epic** p____ f__ example, t__ __he convention of the **epic hero's** descent into hel__ __n much love poetry, the loved one is described in conventional ways. A clic__ ___erry *lips*—ugh—for example) is a convention that has died of overuse.

d__actic poetry— verse that strongly advocates a point of view (e.g., **political poetry**) or aims to teach ___ __ience (e.g., __oral poetry)

dramatic poetry— verse that is meant (____ __ppropriate) for performance by actors

elegy—a poem of
amentation or
sorrow

[epic]—a long
[poem with] telling
[a story] how a
community or
nation came to be
formed. A central
figure called the
[hero] faces the
[?] nature
[?] in [?],
[a]nd [?] life and
limb in other
conventional ways
to bring the
community into
being.

genre—a type or
kind of literature,
poetry, or art: for
example, comic,
epic, or tragic
poetry. Each genre
[?] to play a
[?]stic form
or subject matter.

light verse—
poetry that [?] [pl]ayful
or humorous. Light
verse is usually
rhymed. [?] sometimes
people speak as if
light verse were
somehow less
important than
other kinds of
poetry. Bunk.

lyric poetry—a
catch-[?] [fo]rm for
short (usually),
personal (usually),
musical poetry. Lyric
poetry normally is
contrasted with epic
poetry (which is
communal in
nature) and
dramatic poetry
which is, well,
dramatic). When
most people think of
poetry, they think of
lyric poetry.

myth—a story that

Network television gives us toilet humor, cable brings streams of curses punctuated by violence, movies blow things up. But when we want to express ourselves as more fully human, as creatures capable of elevated thought and means of expression—then we have few places to turn. Poetry books may seem out of reach to some, but hearing a poem read is soothing and healing and helps to put us in touch with our true feelings.

And when we hear a poem read, we participate in an ancient tradition that ties us to our ancestors and to our community.

This box is meant to provide a sampling of some of the best poems in English of the twentieth century. It draws from the most prominent audio collections in the country: Caedmon, the Library of Congress, *New Letters On The Air* (a syndicated radio literature series of which I was producer and host for 13 years), Watershed, and many other private and public collections.

Certainly, the voices of the towering figures of poetry are in this box, but other poets are still relatively young: whether their work will be celebrated 100 years from now remains to be seen.

More important, and interesting, the twentieth century American poetry community in all its diversity of style and participation is represented. There are the modernists (Williams, Pound, etc.) and their successors the postmodernists (whatever that means); the free verse poets (just about everybody these days) and the believers in rhyme, the New Formalists (nobody wants to be called this); the Language poets (John Ashbery); the Beats (Allen Ginsberg, Jack Kerouac, and Anne Waldman); the feminists (May Sarton and Sylvia Plath); the lesbian feminists

Photo © Dorothy Alexander

Carolyn Forché

(Adrienne Rich and Audre Lorde); and the overtly political writers (Marge Piercy, Muriel Rukeyser).

There are funny poems to be found here (Ogden Nash, Lawrence Ferlinghetti, David Ray), and ironic ones (e. e. cummings, Charles Simic); sad poems (Carolyn Forché, Rita Dove, James Ragan) and lots of love poems (Richard Wilbur, Robert Penn Warren); poems with an edge (Charles Bukowski); lush poems (Richard Howard, Derek Walcott); poems read to music; poems written with and without rhyme or meter. Some of the poems are written by Christians (Donald Revell), some by Jews (Dan Jaffe), and others by Zen practitioners (Gary Snyder).

But perhaps the most exciting development in this box, and in contemporary poetry as a whole, is the increasing participation of minority voices. Clearly, poetry is no longer the sole province of white men. Choosing a number of fairly young, minority poets for this box was a conscious decision and a reflection of what I find most exciting and engaging in literature today. Always, I have felt that my first obligation was to great writing and that great writing is best served by those with something fresh and challenging to say. More than any other writers, those of color have the ability to introduce us to new worlds, new ways of seeing the world, and exciting ways to use language.

African-American writers have long been important figures in American poetry, and one of those represented here, Langston Hughes, is an established poetry giant. (Alas, Gwendolyn Brooks would not give permission to include her work.) Rita Dove, a Pulitzer prize-winner and former Poet Laureate, writes about the massacre of blacks in the Dominican Republic by then-President Miguel Trujillo. Maya

Charles Bukowski

examines or explains the universe, a cul[...] or persistent and profound human questions or truths. Some well-known examples are the [...] Icarus and [...], Paul Bunyan and Superman.

narrative poetry—verse that tells a story

occasional poetry—poems written for specific occasions, such as births, deaths, marriages, battles, and invitations to supper

Old English—the earliest recorded version of English, spoken from before the 50[...] to s[...] after the 100[...]. Also called **Anglo-Saxon**, this is the language of *Beowulf* and other fine poetry. Many of the shor[...]crete, gruff [...]s in English—*stone, man, house, knife*—are from Old English.

After the French invaded England in 1066, English c[...] rapidly. Middle English was spoken between 1100 and about 1500, Early Modern English between 15[...] 1750, and after about 1750 or so, just plain Modern English.

parody—a poem (or other kind of art) that makes fun of another poem (or other kind of art) **periods**—For convenience, we imagine history as being divided into periods, within which writers and artists are supposed to have something in common. Yes, this practice is a fiction of convenience. Chaucer would have been surprised to hear that he was *medieval*. We've created periods to help us understand history and how poetry fits in. Here are some of the major periods of English and world literature, along with the length of time they cover. (These are my wildly approximate guesses, because almost everybody disagrees.)

Homeric—1000 B.C. to about 750 B.C.

Classical—750 B.C. to A.D. 476

Dark Ages—476-1000

Medieval—1000-1450

Renaissance—1450-1660

Enlightenment—1660-1798

Romantic—1798-1832

Victorian—1832-1901

Edwardian—1901-1910

Modern—1910-1945

Postmodern—1945 - present

And there are subdivisions and

Angelou contributes her anthem for black women, and Al Young, Amiri Baraka, and Michael S. Harper all take inspiration from jazz.

Participation by Native Americans is a more recent advent on the poetry scene, despite the fact that probably no group of people has an older oral tradition. Here, you'll hear American Indian poets in a frank discussion of the clash between the ancient world and the one in which they live now: Joy Harjo on Anna Mae Pictou Aquash, an American Indian Movement member who was killed by the FBI (Harjo also plays the saxophone on this track); Adrian Louis on alcoholism among Indians; and Luci Tapahonso—who often writes about Navaho ritual—with a charming and hilarious poem about a young woman in a bad relationship with an Indian cowboy.

Four Latino writers read in this collection, among them Jimmy Santiago Baca, who learned to read and write while in prison, and Luis Rodriguez, who took up poetry after leaving a Los Angeles street gang. Carmen Tafolla has a Ph.D. but tells of her troubles with speaking English as a second language.

The youngest poet included is Indonesian-born Li-Young Lee. Lee's grandfather was the personal physician to Mao Tse-tung and his father a Christian revival preacher who was jailed in Jakarta and later moved to the United States. Lee's poem, "My Father, In Heaven, Is Reading Out Loud," sounds at times like the thoughts of any young man who feels himself a disappointment to his father, at other times, like the true experience of an exile:

> . . . but I don't disparage scholars;
> my father was one and I loved him,
> who packed his books once, and all of our belongings,
> then sat down to await instruction
> from his god, yes, but also from a radio.
> At the doorway, I watched, and I suddenly
> knew he was one like me, who got my learning
> under a lintel; he was one of the powerless,

*to whom knowledge came
while he sat among
suitcases, boxes, old
newspapers, string.*

Joseph Brodsky

The only poem not originally written in English in this box was also written by an exile. Joseph Brodsky came to America after serving time in prison in his native Russia. Here, he won the Nobel Prize and was named Poet Laureate (a job he loathed, calling it "ill-defined and underpaid"). I included Brodsky long before his recent death because the idea for this collection came out of a brainstorming session he and I had in a hotel room in Aspen, Colorado, during the summer of 1991. A year later, when I presented the idea to Richard Foos, the founding president of Rhino, he (much to my amazement) liked the idea and decided to act on it. Getting from there to here has been an enormous task, but one well worth the effort.

My hopes for this collection are many: Mostly, I want it to bring pleasure and to stir all sorts of emotions; then, I hope it will give a strong overview of what the last century of poetry has been like. Finally, it should prompt further interest in poetry and in language—an interest that will translate itself into reading and writing and reverence for the great gift of self-expression through words. And the better we are able to express our thoughts, ideas, fears, and emotions, the better we'll be able to communicate with—and perhaps even love— one another.

—*Rebekah Presson*
1996
dedicated to my husband Dewey F. Mosby

sub-subdivisions.

satire—a poem (or other kind of artwork) that holds up a particular social be███ or ridicule for the purpose of amendment

tragedy—a poem (or other artwork) that explores human limits by recounting the downfall of an admirable but flawed figure (the **tragic hero**). Tragedy explores how character is fate and vice versa.

verse—another word for *poetry*. Sometimes the word *verse* is used to disting███ ered, rhymed poetry from other kinds. The word *verse* may also mean

• a single **line** of poetry
• a single **stanza**
• **light verse**
Verse, is what it could be.

45

"Words You Might Hear Other People Use When They Talk About Poetry" excerpted from the book ██ould Be Verse, ███y ██y's Guide To Poetry, by *John Timpane. Available at your local bookstore. Or order from Ten Speed Press 1-800-841-2665.*